Words, after Words, after Words:

POETRY, PROSE AND PROVOCATION

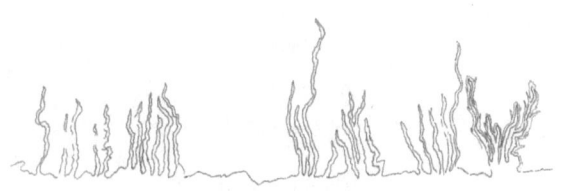

Shreeya Jhaver

BLUEROSE PUBLISHERS

India | U.K.

© Shreeya Jhaver 2024

All rights reserved by author. No part of this publication may be reproduced, stored in a retrieval system or transmitt any form or by any means, electronic, mechanical, photocopying, recording or otherwise, without the prior permissi the author. Although every precaution has been taken to verify the accuracy of the information contained herein, publisher assumes no responsibility for any errors or omissions. No liability is assumed for damages that may result the use of information contained within.

BlueRose Publishers takes no responsibility for any damages, losses, or liabilities that may arise from the use or misu the information, products, or services provided in this publication.

For permissions requests or inquiries regarding this publication,

please contact:

BLUEROSE PUBLISHERS

www.BlueRoseONE.com

info@bluerosepublishers.com

+91 8882 898 898

+4407342408967

ISBN 978-93-6783-091-8

Cover and book design by Deepa Kamath
All photographs and sketches by Shreeya Jhaver, except for
three images of Shreeya from the family collection

First Edition: October 2024

To Mumma, Ma and Nani,
the strongest women I know.

Thank you for being my inspiration.

Contents

'Good artists borrow, great artists steal.' 1

Here I am, Read Me • 5

***to*words 10**
Alliteration • 13
An Apology to My Verses • 16
The Hypocrisy of the Alphabet • 18

***sea*words 22**
The Bay of Bengal • 25
Colours: The Sky Cries in Tinted Tears • 27
A Human • 30
Red • 31

in*word*s 37
Mining for Treasure • 39
The Examiner • 41
Three Feet Thinker • 48
Quiet • 51

back*words* 57
The Tree Stump • 59
Lines • 61
The Library • 63
A Reader's Romance • 67
I Live • 69
The Entire World;
I see the world in a speck of dust • 71
Wondering out Loud • 73
Please, Please Don't Touch My Book • 74

on*words* 80
Unnamed • 83
Ascent • 85
Descent • 87
Teacher • 89

Meet the Author • 93
Acknowledgements • 94
Endnotes • 96

'Good artists borrow, great artists steal'

And so this title was stolen. Francis Picabia was a French artist, illustrator, writer, editor and poet whose first definitive publication released in English (translated ingeniously by Marc Lowenthal) was titled *'I Am A Beautiful Monster: Poetry, Prose and Provocation'*. Much like Picabia's perplexing and polemical poems and his radical, non-conformist art, this book is an open expression of the raw emotions associated with 'feeling' or 'creating' something new. Although naive, it is inspired by the incessant and vitally important *need* to write.

To me, this book is a journal of my writing, chronicling moments of significance, but more so those that are deemed insignificant, home to writing of all kinds—good and bad, each piece equally a part of its identity. These are voices that rebel, react, rebirth, and revive themselves in words, a compilation of living beings. They are stories that have grown with time, fermented and changed colour—they have transformed and been translated into new tongues, taken new titles and torn across novel experiences in a torturous but transfixing process. This is my first attempt at making meaning of maddening things and it spins in a multitude of diverse directions. Yet, words are intrinsic to and embedded in each of these disparate pathways; they all lead back to each other and to home.

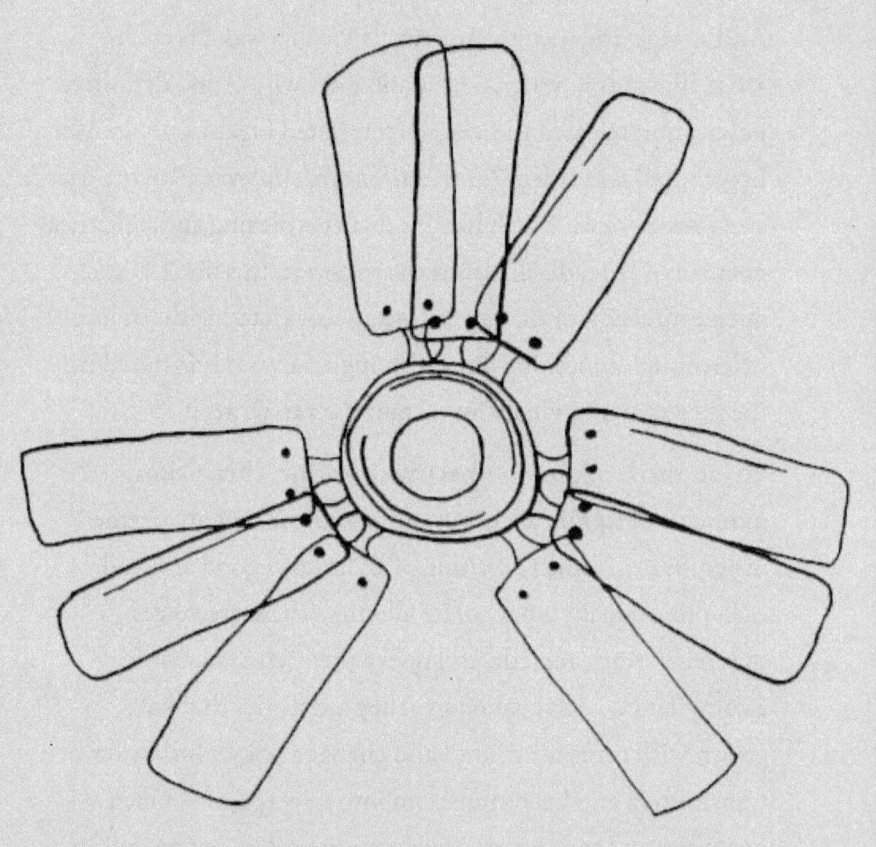

'Our heads are round so our thoughts can change direction.'

FRANCIS PICABIA

Here I am, Read Me

Here I am,
hands shivering, skin trembling at the thought that my retinas
will be pierced by yours,
Scared that my sacred secrecy will never return.
And though these intrepid footsteps mask
The uncertain knees
That have shrunk like a waning moon,
Inside the organs, hell breaks loose.
It's dark in there,
Where ligaments tug and rip,
And panic flourishes its whip,
Beating the ends of my sinews.
Its frigid inside, although perspiration still rides
Like a lone traveller, on the steep curve of my back.
Still, I say, Here I am.
You can read my poetry,
I'll open my mouth wide,
And you can come and look inside
As the epiglottis flails,
And the words rise above,
From the place in which I hide the behemoth.

And I'm scared for you to see,
But still, I say, here's my poetry,
And stand there and smile,
Chest pumping like a missile on the ribcage,
Vessels of blood, running amuck,
As I stand there and let you turn the page.

'I am out with lanterns,
looking for myself.'

EMILY DICKINSON

*to*words

This section is an ode to writing, brimming with words that have fallen on the far side of a glass window with infuriating ignition, that have filled lakes and ponds and rivers and now flood the ocean. Too many words are not always a good thing but they have always been an innate part of my identity. In celebration of the excess, the imbalanced and the abstruse, this section is dedicated to the elements that enable and inspire us. These are poems written *to* the foundations of writing— *to words*.

Alliteration

Poetry is messy,
Full of minute, mellow, meandering pieces,
Of turning, twisting words,
Telling terrific tales,
Of turbulent journeys,
And tired travellers.
All they ever did was try.
Tried to trespass the alien landscape where they found home,
Traverse that treacherous trail,
Toy with the tempestuous waters,
Trek the temperamental terrain,
Where there's sunshine, and rain,
moonshine and clouds
Shrouds of doubt,
Shredded, shallow, shameless thoughts,
Shadowing the shackled truth.
The tiring, tormenting, troubled truth
Tying authenticity to sensitivity,
With opulent ornate ornaments,
Onomatopoeia, alliteration,
Pretty, polished, peripheral words,

Preaching, pretentious, pernicious words,
Pretending words, and alliteration.
To make you reconsider, your revered, repeated thoughts,
To make you wait before delivering your pregnant retorts,
Restless retorts,
Determinedly, deliberately, delivering,
Your pervasive, pregnant, restless retorts,
Words that are a pittering, pestering, penetrating pandemic,
Shaking, shouting, sheltering,
Hurting, hugging, hurtling,
Sowing, seeing, streaming.
These confusing confounding, creating words that say many things can be true at once,
Wreaking havoc, helplessness, holes, hell in your head.
These words.
These, authentic, auspicious words.
All they do is wonder,
If they might mesmerise and metamorphosize your mind,
Your mesmerising, melodic, mysterious mind,

These alliterating, alternating words,
Their soft, shy shapes,
The garmented, unravelling, hidden truth,
Might it reach you,
Make you detour, discuss and debate, your disarrayed,
disoriented, determined, rightfulness.
Poetry in its prideful, passionate, pure place,
With its alluring, amusing, astounding arms,
May it mind you, meld you, mould you,
fight, fold, find you
In its authentic alliteration.

An Apology to My Verses

There is a free flowing sea,
That resides deep within me,
In whose waves I find my own
Ability to articulate.

In it's salt water,
I sometimes get lost,
So poetry can not always be as,
Shocking, captivating, ornate and alluring,
As I would hope.
For the water in which I write,
Is also the one in which I live.
Sometimes I have to write about the subdued subtleties of mundane thought,
Write for my breath,
Not for my verses to be read,
By people above this water level.

The ornaments feel heavy sometimes,
I yearn to remove the jewellery,
For the world is so different with a naked neck.
These lines, they too get tired,
of clothes.
This is an apology to my verses,
Because I can't always be sure,
And the revolutionary rhymes,
Are on holiday.

Today I write as myself,
A tale neither terrific nor traumatic,
Today, I tell the story,
Of my life under the water,
And the things I see,
I call poetry.

The Hypocrisy of the Alphabet

A for apple, by for ball, u for umbrella, t for tall,
I learnt the song word for word,
Every letter,
Like a bird, that flew out of a closed window.
Syllables I was taught to string,
Together like an offering, to the divine deities of imagination.
To think my own,
To speak my own,
The alphabet of liberation.
In this passion,
There was fire,
To be, to live, to yearn, to desire,
To feel, to mean, to mend, to make,
After every mistake, that pushed in a nail,
I'd come back to the letters and pull it out.
To share, to show, to shame, to shout,
But then,
Soon it came to be,
That writing was a necessity.
And the holes the nails left empty,
Were marks that were now being read,

My story, incomplete,
In the words that I'd said.
You ticked or crossed, flicking your fingers,
And like tired soil,
I was no longer fertile,
Dried up and undone,
A became acceptable,
B, below average; euphemism for bad,
C, catastrophic, calamity stricken, sad,
D, dreadful, don't worry, but there isn't much hope,
And your unfeeling 'feedback' cut through my rescue rope,
Don't teach me anything if you're going to make more holes.
For the little water I have is seeping out of them.
Return to me the alphabet you stole,
The illiteracy of illusive imagination,
Illustration,
Illuminating thought.
Oh how I miss them.

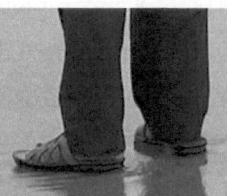

'I am rooted, but I flow.'

VIRGINIA WOOLF

*sea*words

This section is the homecoming.

In the voyage that 'coming of age' is, there is a root that pulls us back, towards the soil.

This section is a dedication to the shore of reason that is also the threshold of discovery.

As I watch the world bend quietly at the frontline and travel beyond with gentle waves of blue nostalgia, it begins to rain. And with the turbulence of change, rain never ceases to fulfil its duty as the bearer of tranquillity. The earth breathes and plumes of petrichor emerge from its exhalations. Within the unrestrained force of falling water, stability emerges and we are readied for transformation. Amidst chaos, we find calm.

The Bay of Bengal

Water has memories of when I stood on your shore,
Rows of waves pulling me towards the brink of your kingdom.
Water has memories of infinity,
Whom we cradled in our arms, just a new born baby.
From where you began,
It seemed the world never ended,
Not even at dusk when we went home.
Water has memories of the time you stole my left slipper,
And hid it in your depths.
I waited barefoot to see if you'd bring it back,
You almost did, but now,
You have that piece of me.
Water has memories of the sky,
Which like a parallel line was never meant to meet you,
But started and ended where you converged with it.
Water has memories of the times you wet the sand on my feet,
And made footprints that you'd wash away,
And then make once again.
For your waves always went back where they came from,
And carried back what they pulled in.
You are my city, my home,

And this salty water,
Knows yours very well,
For the stones that break to make this finely powdered sand,
Bring me back to you.

Colours: The Sky Cries in Tinted Tears

The rain I see is crimson,
Like the *bindi* on the forehead of the dancer,
Droplets that run wild in rhythm,
Beating the surface of the soil,
Like her feet that strike the floor with steadiness,
Her giggling *ghungroos* and their outbursts of excitement,
As soon as her heels touch down,
tiny droplets that jump up,
Before seeping into the soil.

The rain I see is mustard,
Like the turmeric that lingers on her fingers,
Seasoning the monsoon meal,
Piquant ground chillies,
And the stainless steel stirrer,
That rotates hurriedly in her pan.
The whirlwind monsoon breeze that—
Turns gentle before it brushes against your skin,
Sprinkle of garam masala,
As its humid air wets you.

The rain I see is green,
Like the dyed river grass of the *chatai*
that these children play on.
Intricately woven threads of water that
Fall in gracious pattern,
These voices of unreasoned laughter,
Raining memories of innocence that appear on the far side,
of these strings of droplets that we intertwine with,
Like carpets of woven patterns.

The rain I see is brown umber,
Like the wet clay these little hands mould,
Storm swept skies clearing,
Newer beginnings,
like seeds that the tiny fingers bury deep,
And the monsoon petrichor,
As a new moment is brought to life.

The rain I see is blue,
Like the mundane stripes on collars,
Of middle aged office going men,
Who hold stacked steel tiffins,
In hands that discreetly yearn to stand on the balcony,
And catch the monsoon mist.
The steadily metered falling droplets,
That in their transparency reveal,
Their occasional rebelling storms,
Like dancing in the rain with long wet hair.
The unfiltered, offbeat music that rings in the heart
Of a strong cup of tea,
And blue bliss,
In the idleness of innocence.

A Human

There is a person,
Who lives under that stone face,
Back arched tall,
Proud lips.
And these broad shoulders,
that carry that cotton sari like few,
Carry the weight of the world too.
That bespectacled face,
those grave eyes,
Don't seem like they've ever cried, but still,
There's a human behind them somewhere.
.

Red

The bangles clink,
Red,
Like the chilli powder that escapes,
From in between her fingers,
Red,
the sodden tomato,
That floats idly on the surface
Of her warm orange broth.
Red,
the reflection of her face
On the stainless-steel stirrer,
Red,
the sun on this searing summer's day,
Seated in the sky
A blushing, ripe mango.

The veins reveal themselves,
Under the folds of her skin,
On the cusp of her turning wrists,
As she stirs the broth.

Red:
crimson blood,
Redder than the blue part of fire.
Her arms twist vigorously, copiously, intently,
birthing a hurricane
Into the pot.

Sweat seeps
Into the block printed borders
Of her cotton sari, which too is-
Red,
A patchwork poem, a story;
the carmine fibre of her will,
the brick solidity of her solitude.
Red,
her hands.

She spins in the folds
Of her whirlwind broth,
Twisting the wrist,
scarlet guilt,
Vermillion passion,

Burnt rage,
Suppressed silence
Scarlet, cerise, cinnabar silence,
It's a strangling silence and
It's all red.

She spins
Red,
With her turmeric stained fingers,
To change,
See the saffron of a new sun
Rising,
Or
to sustain, to cope –
To be vulnerable in her vigour,
Or then,
Gently forego control,
And let the Red paint her,
Redder than crimson blood,
Redder than the blue part of fire,
Redder than red.

'We've got to live, no matter how many skies have fallen.'

D H LAWRENCE

In words we store fear and frustration yet seek fulfilment too. They conceal our fragility and promise fidelity. We are always heaving sacks of words inside us, and as they are enriched with experience, they grow heavier. We are left hauling them up stairwells and hurtling them across teeming roadways. So, I think healing is reaching down the cavity in your throat, picking words out of the rucksack and throwing them across the room. These poems are a view, through a microscopic lens, of the cosm inside and the chasms within it—a celebration of the uncertainty, anger and dismay that become the catapult with which words are propelled.

in*words*

Mining for Treasure

Outside the bars of my window,
I can see a pair of hands.
Dirty nails,
Mining for treasure,
In a pit of sand.

And I think of the monster that I have become;
My life is all astray.
I see me, the ugly duckling,
Waddling through a storm,
And the swan still seems far, far away.

Somehow all these choices,
Subjects, clothes and books,
Rights and wrongs and morals,
Perceptions and judging looks,

Have made a newfound chamber,
In my unassuming brain.
While I accept the good luck and wishes,
Smiling, though in vain.

God made me too many people,
I wonder which to be.
Even in my shadow,
I don't know which one of me I see.

Wasn't I those children outside the window?
I can't say that I am sure.
Who was I before becoming,
Candidate 2 3 3 4?

What happened to the lion's laugh,
And the fiery eyes?
The honest stubborn glares;
Tamed,
And suddenly wise?

I see this long, long road ahead,
Like a ball of wet clay.
I must shape and mould it,
Pottery isn't for play.

The Examiner

I suspect there is an examiner,
Anonymous and unknown,
For whom we write our stories,
For whom I write this poem,
For whom we pride our authenticity,
In a world where some do lie,
For whom we show integrity,
For they know the purpose of our whys,

But not because we're fearful,
Not because he's keeping score,
But because someone knows your narrative,
Because there is somebody who saw,

Because he lies in the nooks and crannies,
The dust suspended in a ray of light,
The pollen in the heart of a flower,
The in-
Significant details,
Brushed away from sight,
That become the nuclei of a new beginning;
Of all that still prevails,

And from these tiny crevices,
He notices when you're right,
Contemplates your mislearnings,
To resee, reflect and relight.
Sees your passion for the things that burn you,
Yet in whose fire,
You appear most bright,

In those ashes he watches reborn,
The reminiscent
Phoenix of light.
There is them, who have compassion,
For your passion; the friction that steadies your flight.
He is them, he is there,
Your unknown anonymous examiner.

Three Feet Thinker

He sits silently on the bench,
Book in his hands,
Back slumped, head down,
And she,
Flexes her legs,
Rotates her ankles,
And asks him to read.
His quiet voice emerges,
Like a tortoise from its shell,
Some words unsure,
And some certain.
She sits beside him,
And takes careful notes,
with a sugary smile.
Asks what this means and that,
And then when he's done, she points at his face,
And explains that he misread line 2 word 3.
You see the word on the page was 'shallow'
But he'd read it out as 'deep'.
And he knows that her smile is too sweet,
Because adults don't take you seriously,
If you don't know what they mean.

To him,
The three feet thinker,
The shallow end of the pool was deep,
He could submerge his mind in waters
That only reached her feet.
And she doesn't know it but he,
Knows that sarcasm seeps,
Through her eyes that speak a different language,
To the ones he knows.

She scans her list and then,
Call another one to the bench,
And the little one reads.
'Out loud' she says,
'So I can hear you',
But the little girl knows,
That she,
Wouldn't 'hear' her even if she screamed,
So in her mind she reads the story,
And out loud, lets the silence be read,

Another one from the list,
Another book off the pile,
And the laptop keeps calculating,
A heartless percentile,
What they know and what they don't,
When they speak and when they won't,
And she rotates her ankles once again,
And thinks of when twenty years ago,
Someone called her to the bench,
Noting down the words that came out uncertain,
And questioning even those that were sure,
Shaking the foundations she had built,
With definitions someone else wrote,
Their eyes level with the land,
And she, head in the water,
Could only pretend to understand.

Quiet

Build the bars before the window,
Until they are the pillars,
On which this freedom stands.
Like handcuffs being removed,
Just to cut off hands.

We say we need peace,
But here there is silence,
And it's quiet ignorance,
Becomes hidden violence.

Humans are expressive animals,
Born with fires inside.
That struggle even when they are extinguished,
Try never to subside.

What is forbidden in the day,
Hides from golden daylight,
Lurks in the shadows of rebellion,
Writes verses to the stars at night.

As the moon struggles out of a cloud,
People shake off the blankets,

That shield the view of the blind,
Cover the ears of the deaf.
And so, at night, revolution reveals itself,

The tongues that have been cut off,
Wriggle out of their ropes somewhere.
They speak stories of their own simplicity,
In a world so full of care.

Don't think that the blind can't see,
That you've put blindfolds on their eyes.
That the deaf can't hear through the censors,
Your sharply constructed lies.

And the mum, you may think they're quiet,
But their voices create storms in the sky.
The whirlwind of words hidden under their wings,
Oh you haven't seen them fly.
Tonight there is quiet.
There is silence and we are still,
But the echoes of a revolution,
Forms in the powers of our will.

'We are the ones we have been waiting for.'

ALICE WALKER

Moving forwards is disillusioning. It evinces an unusual sense of joy that seems to almost immediately reverse itself.
    When the world flips around, and acrobatically changes direction, as if an independent spindle is suddenly spinning it clockwise rather than counterclockwise, retrograde instead of prograde, forwards becomes backwards. In memory, in nostalgia, in the past, there is a distinctive charm that begins all beginnings. These are the first poems written for this book, bottled in time like scattered souvenirs. As we shift perspectives and flip backwards, these become the relics that were written for words that now bring us back to words—to ourselves, when we need it.

back*words*

The Tree Stump

Haven't you heard that even the hemlock,
Loses its leaves?
And when its needles fall onto the ground,
They aren't quite as green.
And if they don't wither on their own,
Lumberjacks cut off their heads,
And though arborists cry at the loss,
They know everything has an end.
Soon the rings on its stool,
Fade away,
Visitors sit on the stump,
And go away,
Even sunlight frowns upon,
The leftover half of a dead tree.
And though arborists are angry,
The assassin isn't to blame,
For this tree and his stump,
Weren't meant to remain.
Ask the path that you're walking on,
Why you can't see beyond the horizon,

For if you could,
You'd know,
That there is a place where it ends,
A place where the ground starts to crack,
And you fall in.
They say the hemlock is evergreen,
But as its rings lose their wisdom to the breeze,
The wood knows that nothing more could have been.
Every fire starts to die,
Either the water of the world,
Or tears from its own eyes.
Though I remember who you were,
And how I felt,
I mustn't walk backwards on a road that's met its end,
Maybe we were hemlock,
But I don't brood over the stump,
I don't think I'll be sitting there,
Waiting for you to come.

Lines

On your palm,
On the creases of your face,
On the nervous forehead,
On the map you drew,
Of a homelike place,
On the bark of a tree,
When the storm wounded its skin,
And when you inscribed,
Your name for him,
On the pages I write,
With notes on the side,
On thoughts that I scribble on the margins,
Outside hospitals,
And inside cemeteries,
Or made by the veins,
on your skin.
At the beginning of stories,
And in-between sentences.
When you're waiting,
Or when you're thinking, akin.
These are lines that meet you,

Feed you,
When you're growing thin,
And your hair is grey,
When the plastered smile
isn't here to stay.
Lines on your bed,
That creases when you wake,
And lines marking every step that you take.
In chapters that you didn't read,
And made by the stem,
That never came to be,
The ambitious future,
Of an unplanted seed.
Lines on my palm,
And yes, lines on yours,
Lines on my heart,
Where capillaries cross,
Lines made by the tunnel,
Where we once got lost.
Lines from your journey,
And my marks on the floor,
Lines that sometimes meet,
Although no one is sure.

The Library

When I smell the library,
Quiet and yet resolute,
It smells of mist, like a candle
That flickers on a rainy day,
Gentle and yet persistent,
its warmth.

Smells of cinnamon,
Which is warm, but a spice,
And ginger which has a fresh bite,
Every time you taste it in teas,
And of candles,
That create nebulous shadows
On these shelved walls.

Smells of dust that danced
On pages,
'Once upon a time',
When grass grew outside
These windows.

But now it's been a century,
That I haven't touched warm wood,
Sparked a flame as my fingers rubbed against
The bark on the pages of a book.

And don't I crave that midnight light,
Shining through white sheets,
Turning pages of a book with surging adrenaline,
Although it has been read and reread for years now,

It has been hugged and held,
For years now.

Don't my hands crave the weight,
Of a well-lived, emotionally aged,
Bundle of pages,
In which to unleash my own fate,
To learn from another,
Not to escape.

It's the one thing in people,
That I have not found,
That lets me live as myself all year round,
In stories of someone else,
But narratives I craft,

And though its been a while,
It smells of mist, like a candle,
That flickers on a rainy day,
Gentle but still persistent in its warmth.
Maybe I'll read again?

A Reader's Romance

It feels as if I've just met a long-lost friend.
I stare at the face with a knowing smile,
And my hand automatically reaches out.

And as we sit together,
Nothing better than alone,
I feel safe,
Like I'm back in a place I once knew,
Like nostalgia.

There is a momentary awkwardness,
I don't really know where to look,
But my eyes find their way back to the tall spine,
And the moment passes.

Soon enough we're lying on the sofa,
And it feels like we've got back
Right where we left off.

He lies in my hand,
And we feel the same we once did,
In the world we once shared,
In which, momentarily, we existed,

As I stroke the creases on his spine,
The ones I've made and know,
I feel the breath of each page,
The cellars of stories they stow,

And the smell of those pages,
Is yet unnamed,
So comfortable,
that it inevitably feels like home.

He is unique,
In his paperback glory,
And no leather jacketed rarity,
Could even compare.

I know him cover to cover,
And I know what's in between,
At the threshold of his meaning,
I know a world of care.

He crafts so much of me, himself,
That I wonder if he's read me too,

It is a love on which,
Nothing can be said,
A story of lost pages,
And the understanding few.

I Live

I live for the pauses in between words,
That haven't yet been filled,
To colour the world in colours,
that lost wonders spilled

I live for the wrongs,
The falls,
The breaks,
The beginnings,

I live so I can try again,
And again,
And again,
And again,
Somewhere in the search for higher heights,
I live so I can journey the righter rights.

I live to find more white spaces,
That I can live to fill,
I'll live till the world isn't perfect,
And the wind is completely still

And then, I'll live for
The worlds I cannot see,
The words I can't understand,
The trees I have not climbed,
The life I haven't planned

The Entire World;
I see the world in a speck of dust

Who is this world I live for,
Who tells me I'm right and wrong,
who makes me smile and breathe and live,
And sees me so much larger than I am,
Who is this world I live for,
That makes me the world itself,
That echoes my tiny voice and makes it strong.

It's funny how I feel like the wind,
When I'm only the dust it blows away.
I can fly and dance,
How important I must be.
But maybe one day,
the wind will blow me away forever,
And I won't be able to dance ever again.
I'll just be dust,
Who can't move or fly,
Who can't tell itself what to do,
or who to be,
or how to be,

Because dust is nothing important,
Nothing at all.

But it's still the dust,
that the wind carries to the sun.
Only the dust,
that dances in a ray of light,
Like the thoughts and wonders that dance in your mind,
Suspended in motion,
In flight,
And you look at me,
Like I'm the stars that waltz at night,
And for a few moments,
I'm everything you see,
I'm not nothing,
Not nothing at all,
I'm the dust that the wind blows away,
But sometimes,
You make me feel like the entire world.

*This poem makes a reference to 'Auguries of Innocence' by William Blake.

Wondering out Loud

Sometimes I wonder,
If I'll be spent,
Just wishing and hoping and wanting,
The things I know I can do,
But don't,
Because I spent yesterday in bed,
And never got up,
To draw the dreams I dreamt at night.
All the magic died,
Because I never birthed it at all.
I wonder if I've got any talent,
If my mind still works on what's never on paper.
What's the use of a free mind, I wonder,
If it's locked up in my head.
And I say to myself with conviction,
That I've got wonders inside me,
But I guess I'll still be empty,
Until the wonders are made.
And I'll forever be waiting for the day,
When my empty insides and I,
Will make the wonders,
I know I can make.

Please, Please Don't Touch My Book

Please, please don't touch my book,
Where it's been held and felt and torn,
Don't consume the pages,
To which I've sung and sworn,

The sacred paper, sagged with food-stains,
And dampened by water wear,
The occasional smudge of blood,
proof of my eternal care.

These marks are not mistakes,
They are the book I've worn,
Where I've lived and died and lived again,
Where some of me was born,

If you *dare* to smell my book,
To stroke the creases on its spine,
You'll have trespassed the part of me,
That is *only, only mine*.

'I don't know what it is like to not have deep emotions. Even when I feel nothing, I feel it completely.'

SYLVIA PLATH

on*words*

As the wind rustles, limbs tussle and turn. When darkness grips, it is all encompassing. In such darkness, that is so purely black, the inception of light is the greatest. And so, creatives keep their eyes closed. Falling and breaking as we stumble across the unlit room, the insides burn an eternal flame that saves us from further injury. And so, in the pain of burning we find undying light. These poems are on intensity, of emotion, expression and enrichment. They are the alimentary tract that follows digestion and ingestion from the exterior stimulus to interior sensitivity. These are the words that we incubate in our minds and then release, onwards into the atmosphere.

Unnamed

A soft, round spherical object
Falls,
Down the gut,
As if down the vertical pipe
Of a gutter,
Propelled by the gravity
Of the situation
It accelerates in its motion,
sinking, sinking,
until it has sunk,
And hit the lever,
And then rises a fever,
Of fumbling, floundering thoughts,
That fill the brain.
And the lens flutters,
And you helplessly mumble words,
But your breath stutters,
So they cannot be heard.
You shiver,
You tremble,
And every vein,

Pumps blood,
As though it's pumping in vain,
And you wonder,
Why am I here, what can I do,
Spilled my talent
Out of measure,
Unlike you,
I don't have awards,
No trophies to shine,
No most of my life,
I've just been standing in line,
To come home.

Ascent

There is a place,
Where sunshine feels like
Viscous honey,
And filters through the subdued leaves,
In the effervescence of its
Amber glow,
That rustles with the quiet breeze,
Skin is bathed in a tinted tan
Of yellow,
Dark brown hair
Is ignited
with auburn life,
Only beauty
On a blemished face
Appears,
Victorious,
And the shadows of a fresh body,
Seem full,
And nothing less or nothing more,
Seems like it could
Make this orange day better,

Don't need anybody to come and say,
'Hey, you look beautiful'
Because,
Through the cloudy windows,
I see a pink flower on dried leaves,
And I know,
This is what it means,
To be alive.

Descent

Dark glass,
Clouded grey,
Lined with invisible panes,
That create this insufferable jail,
Reflected ceiling lights,
On the surface of the night,
Like a surgical room,
And that hospital white, and don't
I crave for the yellow,
Of unmoved lawns,
The glinting light,
Of melting dawns,
Where the sun loses its form,
And the sphere itself is torn,
Like the bottom of my heavy brain,
That has rained,
Into this body.
I didn't know this private pain,
Would be so physical.
I didn't know that I would see,
Blurred words in bright red,

Surrounding me as I speak.
I didn't know I would hear,
The Scarlett whirring of a fan
In my sleep.
Time is danger,
Danger is deep,
Like the pool of crimson,
Inside my skin,
My blood, my breath,
Seeps in scattered spurts,
Escape is thin.

Teacher

I don't know how to describe such a feeling,
So gentle,
So soft,
So strong.
When I enter those gates confused,
Unnerved,
Unsure,
Bemused,
The earth and the sun,
Are put into one,
just so I can hold my own.
Every footstep rings,
Like the keys of untuned instrument,
Careful where they tread:
They falter as they try
to find their song.
I avoid the eyes,
Dodge the bullets,
And with a shield across my chest,
I walk in bronze,
A knighted stranger.

Flutter away, if I feel in danger,
Hide,
A shy one's plight,
For I wouldn't know what to do
if I were seen.
But you make me feel
Like this unclaimed land,
untravelled and unknown,
Is yours enough to be mine to
call some kind of
home.
I've learned to listen,
Where I should've talked,
Learn, where I would've taught,
And it feels a little different,
The way I sleep tonight.
I dream I'm deep inside an ocean,
Sinking underwater,
Towards solace, and
feeling incredibly light.

Maybe you've made me reach
the dream,
The deep
Fall into my flight.

Meet the Author

I'm Shreeya Jhaver, a seventeen-year-old literary enthusiast with a passion for art, illustration, books and poems. I believe in the importance of self expression and its unyielding power. This book has become a palimpsest of my expression: my thoughts, reflections and stories.

Terry Tempest Williams said, "I write because I do not believe in words. I write because it is a dance with paradox. I write because you can play on the page like a child left alone in sand." Maybe I don't believe in words either, or maybe I believe in them with such conviction that I know they are make believe. Like a child, I make castles and coliseums and cities, filling the world in the cup of my hand. Yet, I know that with sunset the forgotten fact will return with delayed dawning and my world will be engulfed by the ocean once again. It is a fact that the shorelines shift every evening, and at sunrise we reconstruct our broken world. I believe in the words that heave meaning and heal feeling, enough to come back to them every morning and rise. As you read this book, I hope you do too.

Acknowledgements

To my village — thank you for being the hearth that raised this wildfire. The warmth, the light, the fulfillment. For sitting down with me and teasing the threshold of possibility over a cup of tea. For care, for conversation, for this community. Thank you for making this journey yours. This process is dedicated to each one of you, without whom it couldn't have ever been.

Deepa aunty, for being a pillar of support and inspiration— for bringing my ideas to fruition and this book to life.

Ms. Seema Kutty for her thoughtfulness and sensitivity in making meaningful revisions and giving this book finesse.

Shivu, for inspiring me with his intrinsic creativity, far out of the box ideas and invigorating energy.

Nanu for his lessons in resilience, grit, grace and fashion. For giving me joy and showing me the meaning of *jijivisha*.

Papa for support, solidarity and steadiness. For teaching me that persistence is to laugh, learn and let go. And so, for persisting in his efforts to keep me laughing.

Mumma, for being the spine that holds these pages together. For making this possible. For being the first to read, review and resonate with these words — for being the reason I ever wrote them. For holding my hand. For making *me* possible.

Nani, Ma, Babaji, Masi, Masa, Sharanyu, Aadyu and all of my friends, for being my stimulus, my sustenance and the reason I smile.

To everybody else who contributed on the way, for helping me realise that self expression is really community expression. Many tales, many eyes, many poignant passersby. Thank you for telling me your stories, lending me your perspectives, challenging me and changing me.

Endnotes

"Auguries of Innocence." *The Poetry Foundation,* https://beta.poetryfoundation.org/poems/43650/auguries-of-innocence. Accessed 7 Oct. 2024.

Carrying Books as a Safety Blanket: Why the Poems of Sylvia Plath and Mary Oliver Have Been My Travel Companions – Kunzum. 5 Nov. 2022, https://kunzum.com/sylvia-plath-and-mary-oliver/.

Connolly, Jim. "Good Artists Copy, Great Artists Steal." *Creative Thinking Hub, 6 Nov.* 2013, https://www.creativethinkinghub.com/creative-thinking-and-stealing-like-an-artist/.

Dickinson/Holland Correspondence: About 20 January 1856 (Letter 182). https://archive.emilydickinson.org/correspondence/holland/l182.html. Accessed 7 Oct. 2024.

Francis Picabia: Our Heads Are Round so Our Thoughts Can Change Direction | The Brooklyn Rail. 19 Aug. 2024, https://brooklynrail.org/2016/12/artseen/francis-picabia-our-heads-are-round-so-our-thoughts-can-change-direction/.

Lawrence, D. H., et al. *Lady Chatterley's Lover ; A Propos of "Lady Chatterley's Lover."* Penguin Books, 1994.

Walker, Alice. *We Are the Ones We Have Been Waiting for: Inner Light in a Time of Darkness.* 1. publ, Weidenfeld & Nicolson, 2007.

Woolf, Virginia. *The Waves.* Reprinted, Penguin, 2000.

Terry Tempest Williams. *Red: Passion and Patience in the Desert.* Pantheon Books, 2001.

*In some cases, the chosen quotes have contentious origins and who they may be authentically attributed to is unclear. In such cases, the authors that have been credited with them are those whose works have inspired their usage in this book.

www.ingramcontent.com/pod-product-compliance
Lightning Source LLC
LaVergne TN
LVHW041618070526
838199LV00052B/3193